ITeachIT
Year 6 English

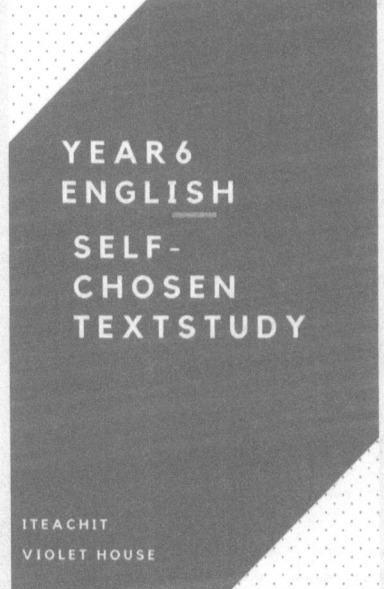

Self-Chosen Text Study

CIP

ITeachIT

Year 6 English

Self-Chosen Text Study

1st Edition

Written by Violet House

First published by Violet House
PO Box 184
Lithgow, NSW, Australia, 2790

Author: Rachel Simone Ford
Publisher: Violet House
Cover Design: Created by Violet House using Canva
Text Design and Typesetting: Violet House
Chapter Opening Images: Created by Violet House using Pages

ISBN 978-0-6488421-1-8

© 2021 Violet House

Copyright notice
COPYING FOR EDUCATIONAL PURPOSES
The Australian *Copyright Act 1968* (Act) allows a maximum of one chapter or 10% of this book, whichever is greater, to be copied by any educational institution for its educational purposes provided that the educational institution (or the body that administers it) has given a remuneration notice to Copyright Agency Limited (CAL) under the Act.

COPYING FOR OTHER PURPOSES
Except as permitted under the Act, for example a fair dealing for the purposes of study, research, criticism or review, no part of this book may be reproduced, stored in a retrieval system, or transmitted in any form or by any means without prior written permission. All enquiries should be made to the publisher at the address above.

For full details of CAL licence for educational institutions contact CAL, 11/66 Goulburn Street, Sydney, NSW 2000. Email: info@copyright.com.au

	1
ITeachIT	1
Year 6 English	1
Self-Chosen	1
Text Study	1
CIP	2
How to use this text	4
Structure	4
Features boxes	6
Curriculum Links	7
The Australian Curriculum: English	7
Self-Chosen Text Study	9
Choosing a text	9
Reading strategies	16
	19
What if?	20
	26
Me, Myself and My text	27
	33
Text recreations	34
	42
Book review	43
	46
Concluding the unit	47
Extension	49
Resource List	51
Suggested texts	51
Appendix	54
Teacher resources	54
Student resources	69

How to use this text
Structure

This resource has been designed to foster a student-centered approach to learning. The activities chosen in the text are designed to engage students in stimulating learning experiences; empowering students to take ownership of their learning and in turn, promote life-long learning.

Each lesson starts with "before you begin". The aim of this section is to:

- Introduce students to new content or learning experiences,

- Connect the content in the body of the lesson to the student prior learning or experiences,

- Prepare the students to learn subject specific knowledge by engaging in warm-up or other activities.

The body of the lesson creates opportunities for the students to generate questions, expand their knowledge and develop their own ideas. This section can also include the explicit teaching of new ideas, knowledge and skills relevant to achieving the identified outcomes of the Australian Curriculum.

The final part of each lesson is a reflection. By reflecting on the lesson, students are provided an opportunity to:

- Consolidate their ideas, knowledge and skills,

- Develop the capacity to self-monitor progress, achievement and areas for improvement or development.

Features boxes

This text features three kinds of features boxes. The first box, in grey, provides additional information for the teacher. This can include definitions of key terms, hints for online or 1:1 learning or additional examples of techniques or information to use with the students.

> Graphics organisers are useful tools for helping students

The second box, in green, indicates that there is additional content for use by the teacher in the teacher resource section of the text.

> There is a selection of reading

The third and final box, in blue, indicates that there is additional content for use by the student in the student resource section of the text.

> A Y Chart can be found in the student resources.

Curriculum Links

The Australian Curriculum: English

Make connections between students' own experiences and those of characters and events represented in texts drawn from different historical, social and cultural contexts (ACELT1613)

Create literary texts that adapt or combine aspects of texts students have experienced in innovative ways (ACELT1618)

Experiment with text structures and language features and their effects in creating literary texts, for example, using imagery, sentence variation, metaphor and word choice (ACELT1800)

Participate in and contribute to discussions, clarifying and interrogating ideas, developing and supporting arguments, sharing and evaluating information, experiences and opinions (ACELY1709)

Select, navigate and read texts for a range of purposes, applying appropriate text processing strategies and interpreting structural features, for example table of contents, glossary, chapters, headings and subheadings (ACELY1712)

Plan, draft and publish imaginative, information and persuasive texts, choosing and experimenting with text structures, language features and digital resources appropriate to purpose and audience (ACELY1714)

Re-read and edit students' own and others' work using agreed criteria and explain editing choices (ACELY1715)

© Australian Curriculum, Assessment and Reporting Authority (**ACARA**) 2010 to present, unless otherwise indicated. This material was downloaded from the Australian Curriculum website (www.australiancurriculum.edu.au) (**Website**) (accessed 21August 2018) and was not modified. The material is licensed under CC BY 4.0 (https://creativecommons.org/licenses/by/4.0). Version updates are tracked on the 'Curriculum version history' page (www.australiancurriculum.edu.au/Home/CurriculumHistory) of the Australian Curriculum website. ACARA does not endorse any product that uses the Australian Curriculum or make any representations as to the quality of such products. Any product that uses material published on this website should not be taken to be affiliated with ACARA or have the sponsorship or approval of ACARA. It is up to each person to make their own assessment of the product, taking into account matters including, but not limited to, the version number and the degree to which the materials align with the content descriptions and achievement standards (where relevant). Where there is a claim of alignment, it is important to check that the materials align with the content descriptions and achievement standards (endorsed by all education Ministers), not the elaborations (examples provided by ACARA).

Self-Chosen Text Study

Choosing a text

Before you begin

Ask the students to reflect on their experiences with literature by using a Y chart.

> Graphics organisers are useful tools for helping students to organise information and thoughts and to simplify complex ideas and new information.

Encourage the students to choose any three of the five sensations to complete the Y chart. For example, they may choose "Looks like… Feels like… Smells like…". It is important that students understand there is no right or wrong answer for their reflection.

Ask the students to share their experiences with you, only if they are comfortable doing so. The students will review the chart at the end of the unit, so they should ensure it is filed/stored in a safe place.

A Y Chart can be found in the student resources.

Lesson

One way for students to engage with literacy, language and literature is to study a text they have chosen themselves.

Before beginning the unit, ask the students to bring a text that they have enjoyed to the lesson. The text can be any mode for example: novel, novella, non-fiction, poem, play, comic, manga etc.

Ask the students to write a short paragraph explaining why they engaged with their chosen text. Try not to restrict the student's answers for this activity, the aim is to encourage the students to identify positive interactions they have had with literature.

If possible, ask the students to show a copy of their text and to read their paragraph. As the students listen to each other, ask them to take note of any similarities or themes that they notice between their text and the texts chosen by their peers using a Venn diagram.

> A Venn diagram can be found in the student resources.

After every student has been given an opportunity to share, invite the students to discuss the similarities and themes they noticed across the self-chosen texts. As a class, or in small groups, discuss why certain themes may be popular amongst the class.

...ents, ask the students to complete the ...rcise for 2 - 5 texts, looking for themes and ...ilarities across the texts.

In preparation for the next lesson, ask the students to find a fiction text that they would like to study.

r students who are unsure about what text to study, th
an extensive suggested reading list in the teacher

Reflection

Before finishing the lesson, ask the students to reflect on what they learnt about their peers reading styles and interests.

As a class, discuss if the students were inspired to read any of the texts mentioned by their peers. As part of the discussion, encourage the students to explain why they were inspired to read the text.

ndividuals, or as an alternative task, ask the dents to discuss what influences them to ose a text to read.

Reading strategies

Before you begin

As the teacher, describe a time that you have read a text based on a recommendation from a friend, book review or another source. In your description be sure to include why you chose to follow the recommendation.

After reading your description, ask the students if they have ever self-chosen a book based on a recommendation. If the students have self-chosen a book based on a recommendation, discuss what influenced their choice.

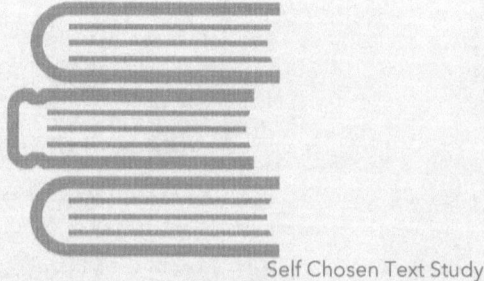

Lesson

Begin by presenting the students with a series of reading comprehension strategies.

Ask the students to choose one of the reading comprehension strategies. After the students have chosen a strategy, they should create a template that they can use for their chosen strategy.

> reading
> comprehensio
> ategies in th
> cher resour
> tion.

> quired, there are a number of templates for
> students to use in the student resource
> ion.

The students should read at least one chapter of their chosen text and complete the template for the reading comprehension strategy. In small groups, or working individually, discuss the advantages and disadvantages the students are finding with their chosen strategy. Once the students have discussed the advantages and disadvantages of their chosen strategy, ask the students to identify steps to overcome the disadvantages.

Over the course of a number of lessons, the students should complete reading their text, creating a summary for each chapter as they read.

Reflection

After the lesson has been completed, ask the students to write a short email to their peers recommending their chosen reading strategy.

What if?

Before you begin

As a class, conduct a discussion based on the following questions:

- Have you ever wanted to change the ending on a movie? Why?

- Have you ever wanted to change the ending of a book? Why?

- What do you think would happen if you changed an ending you are not happy with?

- What do you think would have happened if you made the changes you wanted?

Lesson

Using their chosen reading comprehension strategy as a starting point, the students should identify the turning point in the story.

choice/s that the protagonist make or the action takes, changes the direction of the story. Examples of a turni point include: a deduction (when the protagonist piec all the evidence together); a test of will (the protagoni gives up something that is important to them or finds courage); an unknown plan (the protagonist signs up t an impossible task, and during the turning point they reveal they had a plan all along); a sacrifice (usually the protagonist gives up their own life, or something equa important to save the rest of the characters/the world) a reward (the protagonist completes a task or work tha

After the students have identified the turning point, ask them to write a short description of what happens. In the description the student should clearly define the rising tension and identify the action/decision taken by the protagonist.

Once completed the students should share their descriptions with other members of the class. As they either listen to, or read each other's descriptions, the students should write a question, starting with "what if" that could change the action in their peer's chosen text.

> ...u are working with a small number of ...dents, or one student, as the teacher you may ...d to create several "what if…?" questions.

For example, the student might ask:

- What if the protagonist turned up to battle but left their weapon at home?

- What if the protagonist sacrificed their sibling instead of themselves?

- What if the antagonist was late to the show down and everyone left?

- What if the antagonist completed the favour for the troll instead of the protagonist's?

After all of the students have had an opportunity to write a question based on the description, the student who wrote the description should read all of the questions posed by their peers.

- Once they have read all of the descriptions the students should choose one "what if…?". Ask the students to rewrite the turning point of the text based on the "what if…" question they have chosen.

may wish to encourage the students to
 their work with their peers and to edit
 other's work. This will provide a "fresh"
 of eyes as well as helping each student to
tice and develop their editing skills.

After creating their own turning point, the students should edit their work. As they edit, they should check their spelling, grammar and punctuation. The students should then perform a second edit of the work, this time reviewing their word choice, checking their tense and looking at how they have constructed their sentences.

Once the students are satisfied with their work, they should publish the work, in an agreed format. Along with the published work, the students should write three to four paragraphs that justify the choices they made in their piece including word choice, action, cause and effect, tension etc.

Reflection

After completing the lesson, ask the students to write a short reflection on any challenges they experienced in rewriting the turning point and how they overcame these.

If the students did not experience any challenges, ask them to reflect on why they enjoyed writing the alternate turning point.

Me, Myself and My text

Before you begin

Either using the list in the teacher resource section, or a list of your own, complete the following:

- Ask the students to find a blank piece of paper and a pen/pencil or open a blank word processing document,

- Inform the students that you will read them a list of words,

- For each of the words the students should write as many events, ideas, images as they can think of,

- Encourage the students not to think and to write down what comes to them without editing.

If time permits, ask the students if they would like to share any experience or idea that they had during the activity.

st of words can be found in the teacher
urce section.

Lesson

Using the reading comprehension strategy as a guide, ask the students to choose one part of the text that they identify with. For example:

- one of the characters and the student may have lost a loved one, someone important to them,

- one of the characters and the student may have achieved a very important goal,

- the location that the text is set in and the student may have experienced an important event or natural disaster.

> There is no limit on what the students may identify with, the goal is to help them identify an overlap between the text and their own

Once the students have chosen the part of the text they identify with ask them to create a recount of the event or situation. The recount should be as factual and logical as possible.

> A recount gives an account of an event or experience.

Collect all of the recounts. Once all of the recounts have been collected, give each student another student's writing. The students should read and record the recount that they are given. As they read the recount, the students should focus on only saying what is on the page that is, they should not add any words that may be missing, or any emotion or inflection.

After all of the students have recorded the recount, collect them and being as objective as possible, the students should listen to the recorded recount to ensure that accurately describes the chosen event for situation. Based on their observation of the recording the students should edit their recount.

Repeat the writing, recording and reviewing of the recount, but this time, the students should use the chosen event or situation from their text as the basis for their writing.

Once the students have edited their recount and are satisfied that both recounts are accurate, they should create a Venn diagram that shows the similarities and differences between their event or situation and the one they choose from their text.

Based on the Venn Diagram, the students should write a short paragraph titled "Me. Myself and My Text".

Venn diagram can be found in the student resources.

Reflection

In small groups, the students should discuss the following statement. In their discussion, they should give examples from the recount they created, as well as any other examples they can think of.

All fiction is a reflection of real life.

Text recreations

Before you begin

As a class, discuss the different types of language and text features the students are familiar with. For example: setting, character, language (metaphor, simile, colloquial, hyperbole, emotive etc), sentence structure. After identifying as many different types of language and text features as they can, ask the students to identify one or two language or text features that they really enjoy.

Working in pairs, ask the students to complete the following thinking skills activity:

A: State the feature that they enjoy.

B: Ask "Why do you like X"

A: Answer B's question.

B: Ask "Tell me more about X".

A: Answer B's question.

B: Ask "Can you give me an example of X".

A: Answer B's question.

B: Ask "Can you tell me more about X".

After completing the sequence above, the students swap so that A asks the questions.

A: I like a book that has a lot of imagery.

B: Why do you like imagery?

A: Because it allows me to make my own picture of the book in my head.

B: Tell me more about why you like making a picture in your head.

A: When I make a picture in my head, I feel like I am pa[rt] of the story, like I could be in that world.

B: Can you give me an example of when you felt like yo[u] were in the story?

A: When I read *The Big Dry* by Tony Davis, there were a lot of descriptions of the town, the heat and the dust.

B: Can you tell me more about the dust?

A: The dust was almost a character in the book, it swirl[ed,] it moved, it was everywhere, always getting in the way.

Lesson

Recreate a section of the text in a different mode. The recreation should stay as close to the original text as possible, whilst also adhering to the conventions of the chosen mode. For example, if recreating the chosen section as a picture book, the student would illustrate key concepts and reduce the amount of text, but at this stage, they would not change any of the literary conventions.

modes may include the following: graphic
l, picture book, poem, textbook, film,
rmance or animation

After recreating a section of the test in a new mode, the students should experiment with changing the language so that it more closely aligns to the mode, without changing the meaning of the original text. For example, the students may choose to experiment with metaphor, simile, alliteration, assonance, rhyme, onomatopoeia or word choice.

Once the students have completed a draft of the text recreation, they should share their work with a peer to read and edit. The editing should focus on spelling, grammar and readability.

If you have an individual student or a small group, then as the teacher you may wish to edit the

Based on their peers suggested edits, and their own re-reading of their work, the students should edit and prepare their work for publication. Once the students are satisfied with the quality of their work, they should publish it in the format that is most appropriate for their chosen mode.

le and may include hardcopy, PDF, eBook,
o file, animation or any other format that is
ropriate.

A metaphor is an expression or statement in which one object is referred to as having similar qualities to anther object. For example: All the world's a stage; My dog Mary is my sunshine; Henry had a heart of stone.

A simile is an expression or statement where an object is compared to another using the words "like" or "as". for example: Mum was as busy as a bee; Andy's voice was smooth like honey; I floated into the room like a cloud.

 Alliteration is the repetition of words that have the same starting letter or sound. For example: the lazy lizard lolled on the log; Chris created a cute kite; Lisa likes licking lollipops.

Assonance is the repetition of vowel sounds in words that are next to each other or close together. For example: grease the squeaky wheel; rhyme nine times; they were here, there and everywhere.

Onomatopoeia is when a word sounds like its meaning. For example: cackle, peep, plop.

Reflection

Using free form writing, ask the students to reflect on the process of recreating a section of their chosen text in a different mode.

Book review

Before you begin

For homework, ask the students to locate and then bring in one or two reviews of their chosen text. In small groups ask, the students to read their review/s and discuss if they agree or disagree with what is written in the review.

ok reviews can be found on
okseller/bookshop websites, in
wspapers and journals, on social
edia and through other sources.

ok reviews can also be found on the
blishing houses' website, but the
dents should be aware of any bias
ay be associated with a review from
urce.

Lesson

For their final task, ask the students to write

> e is a scaffold for a book review in the student
> urce section.

In writing the review, the students should include both the positive and interesting aspects of the book as well as anything they didn't like or engage with. All discussions should be supported by evidence.

The students should draft, edit and then publish their review as if it was going to be published in a print magazine.

Reflection

As a class, discuss why people read and value other peoples' decisions before making purchases such as books, movies, technology etc.

Concluding the unit

Ask the students to reflect on their experiences with literature after completing the unit, using a Y chart. Encourage the students to choose any three of the five sensations to complete the Y chart. For example, they may choose "Looks like… Feels like… Smells like…". It is important that students understand there is no right or wrong answer for their reflection.

Ask the students to review the Y chart they completed at the beginning of the unit and compare it to the Y chart they have just completed. Using any method of their own choice, ask the students to note any similarities and differences between the two Y charts.

Extension

Choose one of the minor characters in the text and tell the story from their point of view.

Create a series of diary entries from the point of view of one the characters.

The features of a diary entry can be found in the teacher resource section.

Write a short story about what happens after the text ends.

Write a short story about what happens before the text begins.

features of a short story can be found in the her resource section.

Create a trailer for a movie version of the text.

her resource section.

Resource List

Suggested texts

The Taylor Turbochaser by David Baddiel

The Fowl Twins by Eoin Colfer

New Kids by Jerry Craft

Barney and the Secret of the French Spies by Jackie French

Barney and the Secret of the Whales by Jackie French

Macbeth and Son by Jackie French

Nanberry: Black Brother White by Jackie French

Pirate Boy of Sydney Town by Jackie French

Invisible in a Bright Light by Sally Gardner

Fire Stallion by Stacy Gregg

Prince of Ponies by Stacy Gregg

Sweet Adversity by Sheryl Gwythwe

Wink by Rob Harrell

The Mystery of the Colour Thief by Ewa Jozefkowicz

Dr Karl's Random Road Trip by Dr Karl Kruszelinicki

Whimsy and Woe by Rebecca McRitchie and Sonia Kretchmar

Boy Giant by Michael Morpurgo

The Girl, the Dog and the Writer in Lucerne by Katrina Nannestad

The Girl, the Dog and the Writer in Provence by Katrina Nannestad

The Girl, the Dog and the Writer in Rome by Katrina Nannestad

Pax by Sara Pennypacker and Jon Kalssen

His Name Was Walter by Emily Rodda

Wakestone Hall by Judith Rossell

Withering-by-Sea by Judith Rossell

Wormwood Mire by Judith Rossell

Bloom by Nicola Skinner

Funny Kid series by Matt Stanton

The Beast of Buckingham Palace by David Walliams and Tony Ross

Fing by David Walliams and Tony Ross

The World's Worst Children series by David Walliams and Tony Ross

The World's Worst Teachers by David Walliams and Tony Ross

Appendix

Teacher resources

Reading comprehension strategies

Storyboard

- Summarises the important information,
- Usually focus on characters and action,
- Uses pictures and short descriptions.

Chapter summary

- Helps to focus on the important information and events,

- Chapter summaries can come in many forms including:

  - 3-2-1,

  - Who, What, Where, Why, How and Vocabulary,

  - First, then, next, finally.

- Usually only contains written information,

Visualising

- If not familiar with visualising, when you first use the technique, start by reading out loud or by having someone else read the text out loud,

- Encourages students to form a 'picture' in their minds of what they are reading,

- Sketches should be quick in order to capture ideas,

- Avoiding using words in the sketch, but if needed, add a description below the sketch.

One sentence summary

• The purpose is to focus on the important information,

• More than one sentence can be written, but each sentence must have a different focus, for example, setting, character, tension, cause and effect, challenge and resolution etc.,

• Strategies such as think, pair, share and peer feedback can be used to refine and improve skills.

Timeline

- Can be horizontal (left to right), vertical (bottom to top) or parallel,

- Can be written, visual or a combination.

- Information can be used to create short summaries,

- Helpful for sequencing events, especially in texts with multiple time sequences.

Suggested word list

Friendship

Loss

Identity

Family

Belonging

Courage

Jealousy

Challenge

Adventure

Magic

Secrets

Love

Strength

Justice

Growing-up

Growing-apart

Anger

Joy

Features of a diary entry

Heading

A descriptive title that will give the reader insight into the entry.

Time stamp

Day, date and time of the entry to help the reader understand the context of the entry.

Language

First person,

Informal,

Usually has a conversational tone,

May include colloquialisms, rhetorical questions, exclamations.

Signature

A signature at the end of an entry can add an element of authenticity.

Features of a short story

Plot

The plot usually consists of three elements: exposition, conflict and denouement:

Exposition: establishing the situation. Exposition may include background, characters, setting and atmosphere.

Conflict: this can also be known as the complication and is the action which the story is centered around. The conflict leads to the climax of the story.

Denouement: the resolution of the conflict (outcome).

Character

In a sort story there are usually two kinds of characters, developing and static.

A developing character undergoes a period of change through the story.

A static character does not undergo a period of change through the story.

Setting

Is usually related to and contributes to the theme,

Helps to create the tone and atmosphere,

Helps the reader to understand the characters.

Point of View (POV)

Usually first person,

    A character in the story,

    Usually central to the action, but may not be,

    Uses the pronoun "I",

Generally omniscient rather than limited POV,

    Generally, the narrator presents a neutral perspective i.e. they do not form sides or give opinions about the course of action that should be taken.

Symbolism

Symbols add impact by creating additional meaning,

Symbols come in many forms including words, objects, sounds, images, characters and concepts.

Theme

A short story will focus on one theme,

The theme is what unifies all elements of the short story,

The theme may be the subject of the short story.

Features of a movie trailer

Feature shots

A movie trailer will use a variety of shots to establish,

The aim of the trailer is to attract an audience, and so the shots chosen are usually the most exciting,

The shots chosen should give some information about the main character, theme and any other important information.

Genre

A movie trailer will help the audience to identify the genre of the film.

Common genres include:

- Comedy
- Drama
- Action
- Fantasy
- Mystery
- Horror
- Romance
- Thriller
- Western
- Science Fiction

Common conventions

Show the "best" parts of the film,

Highlight popular actors,

Chosen shots are short,

Conversations are usually limited to one line,

Action is interrupted by other shots or the credits,

A voiceover may guide the audience and give them information,

Dramatic action builds to the end of the trailer,

The title of the film may not appear until the end of the trailer.

Student resources

Y chart

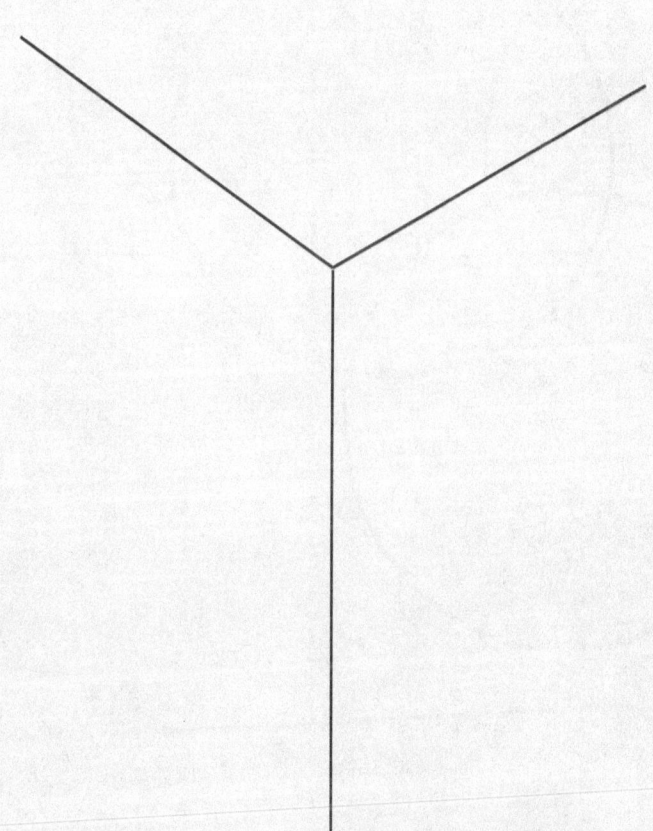

Venn diagram

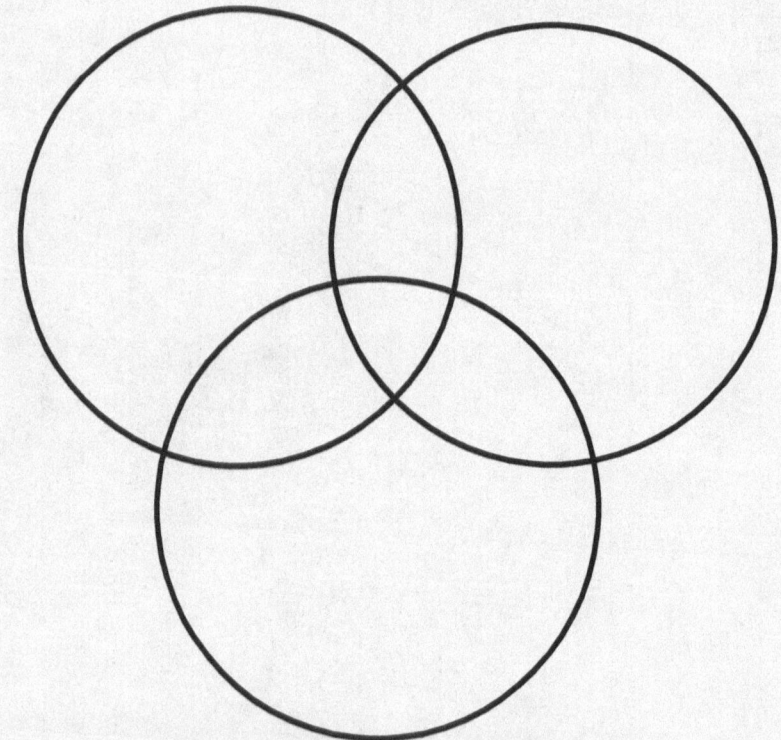

Storyboard

Chapter title/number	Chapter title/number	Chapter title/number	Chapter title/number
Illustration	Illustration	Illustration	Illustration
Explanation/ discussion	Explanation/ discussion	Explanation/ discussion	Explanation/ discussion

Chapter summary

Chapter number/title	Relevant information
First	
Then	
Next	
Finally	

Visualising

One sentence summary

Chapter number/title	One sentence summary

Timeline

Book review

Book title and author	
Description of the book/summary (make sure you don't give away the ending or any important plot twists)	
What did you like about the book: favourite character, favourite part of the book, emotional affect on you, anything else	
Anything you didn't like about the book: character you didn't like, events you didn't like, content you found difficult, anything else.	
Summary	

www.ingramcontent.com/pod-product-compliance
Lightning Source LLC
Chambersburg PA
CBHW021950160426
43195CB00011B/1306